In Praise

In Praise

Art in its many forms is an important part of worship. This volume of *In Classical Mood* concentrates on Christian music as a vital element in the development of the European tradition—from the contemplative 6th-century Gregorian Chant, to the uplifting "Sanctus" from Duruflé's 20th-century *Requiem*. Even Schubert, who was not a religious man, imbues his *Ave Maria* with a spiritual quality, and there is no doubting Haydn's faith in the rejoicing of "The Heavens Are Telling the Glory of God" from his oratorio *The Creation*. This volume draws on the immense range of Europe's religious music and offers a wide variety of works—to those who share the faith and those who are simply inspired by beautiful sound.

THE LISTENER'S GUIDE – WHAT THE SYMBOLS MEAN

THE COMPOSERS
Their lives... their loves.. their legacies...

THE MUSIC
Explanation... analysis... interpretation...

THE INSPIRATION
How works of genius came to be written

THE BACKGROUND
People, places, and events linked to the music

© MCMXCVIII IMP AB   In Classical Mood™   IMP AB, produced under license by IMP Inc.   Printed in China.   US P 2201 12 032

Contents

FRANZ SCHUBERT *1797–1828*

Ellens Gesang No. 3

"HYMNE AN DIE JUNGFRAU" D839: AVE MARIA

Schubert clearly entered into the spirit of "Ellen's Song"—her "Hymn to the Virgin." Well-known as "Ave Maria," from its first words, the prayer's gently flowing and beautiful melody imparts a tone of uplifting devotion. Originally written in 1825 for solo voice and piano, it has been arranged in many different ways: for choir and organ, for voice and orchestra, and for a string ensemble, as heard here.

ACCLAIM FOR MARY

Surprisingly, Mary is not a leading figure in the Gospels. But, as Christianity spread, often through the devotion of women, and to peoples familiar with the female deities of other religions, Mary's importance grew. She is now deservedly revered by most Christian traditions.

THE LADY OF THE LAKE

The text of "Ellen's Song" comes from Sir Walter Scott's epic poem, *The Lady of the Lake*. The Lake is Loch Katrine in Scotland (*above*) near which Ellen and her father—16th-century outlaw, James of Douglas—are being sheltered by Roderick Dhu, a Highland Chief who has fallen in love with her. Ellen, however, loves another, her sweetheart Malcolm. Meanwhile, the King of Scotland, disguised as James Fitz-James, arrives at Dhu's castle. Tragedy looms as the army arrives to arrest James of Douglas who surrenders himself, realizing the game is up. Ellen discovers that Fitz-James is the King in disguise and manages to secure a pardon for her father, before finally marrying her true love, Malcolm. Her song, "Ave Maria," is a plea for Mary to hear a maiden's prayer and to grant her and her father divine protection.

THE MAGNIFICAT

One of the best-loved hymns connected with the Virgin Mary is the *Magnificat*. It is based on words spoken by Mary as recorded in Luke's Gospel. Mary has just heard that she is to give birth to the Son of God. She visits her cousin, Elizabeth, who is also pregnant. When they meet, the child—who is

to become John the Baptist—leaps for joy in Elizabeth's womb. At this, Elizabeth realizes that Mary is to be the mother of the Son of God and pays homage to her (*above*). They are both elated and Mary recites her famous prayer of humility, which begins "My soul doth magnify the Lord."

K E Y   N O T E S

Schubert composed music for eight poems from The Lady of the Lake. Most of them, including all three of "Ellen's Songs," were first sung by his friend, baritone Johann Michael Vogl.

GIOACHINO ROSSINI *1792–1868*

Stabat Mater

CUJUS ANIMAM

This is the second section of Rossini's *Stabat Mater*, his setting of the poem about Mary at the foot of the cross. It tells of her weeping heart (*Cujus animam*) and her grief at the pains of her Son. After a dramatic beginning, the strings introduce an uplifting melody, which is then taken up by the tenor in his opening verse. Later in the aria, Rossini returns to this theme, before building dramatically to a passionate high note that is as much operatic as sacred—demanding a wide range for the tenor voice. The music then regains its former composure and the piece ends on a note of tranquillity.

ROSSINI'S FAITH

Rossini was known as a great wit and entertainer. When someone questioned his religious faith, he said, "Would I have been able to write the *Stabat Mater* and the Mass (*Petite messe solennelle*) if I had not had faith?" However, during his last illness in 1868, he rebuked the Virgin Mary for not relieving his pain.

UNWELCOME COMMISSION

On a trip to Madrid in 1830, Rossini was introduced to King Ferdinand VII of Spain. The King's minister, Fernandez Varela, suggested that Rossini write a setting of *Stabat Mater*. Rossini was reluctant because of his respect for the famous 1736 version by Giovanni Pergolesi (*below*), but was eventually persuaded. Becoming ill, he wrote only part of the piece and asked a friend to complete it secretly. This version was performed in Madrid in 1833. In 1837, however, Varela died and, to Rossini's horror, the score was sold to a publisher. He had the courts prevent it being published and decided to finish the missing movements himself. This genuine version premiered in 1842.

FRANCISCAN POEM

The *Stabat Mater* has become part of the Roman Catholic liturgy for Good Friday, the day commemorating Christ's crucifixion. It was originally a poem attributed to Jacopone da Todi (1230–1306), an Italian monk, and is regarded as one of the greatest works of medieval literature. Along with Rossini and Pergolesi (*left*), Vivaldi, Haydn, Verdi, Palestrina and Dvořák also set this sad text to music.

KEY NOTES

Rossini was very superstitious. This, he said, was due to his uncommon birthdate—February 29. Just before he died, on Friday, November 13 ,1868, he claimed he was only 19!

WOLFGANG AMADEUS MOZART *1756–1791*

Ave verum corpus

K618

The *Ave verum corpus* is a short poem: "Hail True Body, born of the Virgin Mary, truly made to suffer, sacrificed on the cross for man." It was written to celebrate the feast of Corpus Christi, during which an elaborate procession in honor of the Eucharist takes place. Only 46 bars long, Mozart's setting is peaceful, with restrained organ accompaniment. Direct and simple, the piece only reaches a more complex texture in the final, gentle climax. Mozart called this sublime music his "little funeral motet."

MOZART AT BADEN

Mozart wrote this setting of the *Ave verum corpus* for the Feast of Corpus Christi at Baden, near Vienna, in June 1791, only six months before he died. Baden is a spa town, which Mozart's wife Constanze, when pregnant, used to visit to take advantage of the healing waters.

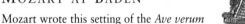

KEY NOTES

Ave verum corpus *was dedicated to Anton Stoll, the influential choir master at Baden Church. At that time, Mozart wrote the "most stupid letter in my life," asking Stoll to book a hotel room for his wife!*

GABRIEL FAURÉ *1845–1924*

Requiem

OPUS 48: PIE JESU

his pure and innocent-sounding solo for a boy treble is a plea to the "sweet Lord Jesus" to give the dead eternal rest. Gently accompanied on the organ throughout, it is first heard with strings and harp, and later with woodwind. It is also the only part of Fauré's *Requiem* to use flutes and clarinets. The pleas for rest rise to a short climax before the hushed singing of *sempiternam requiem*, or "eternal rest."

A FUTURE STAR

Fauré wrote the "Pie Jesu" with the voice of the 10-year-old Louis Aubert in mind. Aubert went on to become a famous pianist and, in 1908, gave the premiere of Ravel's *Valses nobles et sentimentales*.

K E Y   N O T E S

Fauré did not compose his Requiem *for anyone specific only "for the pleasure of it." Begun in 1877, it took until 1890 to reach its final form.*

JOHANN SEBASTIAN BACH *1685–1750*

Cantata

BWV80: EIN FESTE BURG IST UNSER GOTT (CHORALE)

B ach wrote many cantatas, each beginning with a choral section known as a chorale. This one is loosely based on a famous Lutheran hymn tune—picked out by trumpets and oboes—known in an English version by the 19th-century historian Thomas Carlyle as "Our God is a Mighty Fortress." A vigorous and joyful rendering telling of God's protection against the Devil pours out in a chorus of praise, soaring above the melody. Bach's painstaking effort has left a rich reward for church and layperson alike.

PROTESTANT ANTHEM

Bach based this cantata on a hymn written in 1529 by German monk and religious reformer, Martin Luther (1483–1546). Luther's teachings spread far and fast through Germany, and the hymn became a rallying cry for his followers. So much so, that in the years after the French Revolution, the hymn acquired the nickname of the "Marseillaise of the Reformation."

THE REFORMATION

Bach wrote this cantata to celebrate the annual Reformation Festival in Leipzig on October 31. This commemorated the day in 1517 when Martin Luther (*below, preaching*) nailed his 95 Theses to the door of All Saints' Church, in Wittenberg, sparking off the Protestant Reformation. He was excommunicated in 1521 for, among other things, criticizing the practice of selling indulgences (religious pardons). Much of northern Germany supported his views, for political and religious reasons, and his supporters, called Lutherans, helped spread his movement to Scandanavian countries. In time, his teachings would gain an even broader appeal. Today, there are more than 7,000,000 Lutherans in the U.S. alone.

BACH AND ROYALTY

In Bach's time, much of central Europe was grouped under the title of The Holy Roman Empire. This was, in fact, a collection of small states, often rivals and frequently at war. Bach had dealings with various rulers of these states, including Prince

Leopold of Köthen (*above*), his patron from 1717 to 1723. The composer also met King Frederick the Great of Prussia (*right*), for whom he wrote his "Musical Offering" in 1745, based on a theme written by the king himself.

ANTONIO VIVALDI *1678–1741*

Gloria

RV589: LAUDAMUS TE

This is a joyous rendering of the third part of the *Gloria* in Vivaldi's most famous choral setting. It comes between more somber, slower sections for full choir; and the two female voices, soprano and alto, emerge here as a refreshing contrast. Heralded by a powerful and uplifting melody carried on strings, they sing just four phrases, "We praise thee, we bless thee, we worship thee, we glorify thee." First echoing each other's words, the voices then join together in perfect unison, complemented by a lively instrumental background. Harmonizing in a blissful duet, they exult in sublime celebration.

VIVALDI THE CHORAL WRITER

Composing works for the girls' choir at Venice's Pietà orphanage usually fell to the choirmaster, Francesco Gasparini. When he retired in 1713, Vivaldi took his place, proving himself to be a more than worthy successor.

KEY NOTES

Vivaldi wrote two settings for the Gloria while teaching at the Pietà. To this day, scholars disagree over which came first. To help resolve the argument, they have even studied the composition of the paper on which each was written, but have yet to come to a definite conclusion.

GREGORIAN CHANT

Salve, festa dies

The poem *Salve, festa dies* or "Hail, Festive Day" was written by the Byzantine poet Venantius Fortunatus (c.540–600) for the procession of the newly baptized at Easter. He sent it to Felix, Bishop of Nantes in France, as a letter in elegiac couplets (sets of two lines of verse). The beautiful opening words are repeated as a refrain or chorus around three couplets which tell of nature rising from its winter sleep at Easter to greet its creator and redeemer, Jesus. The rebirth of spring with the flowers and trees bursting into life—a theme familiar to monks with their monastery gardens— inspired new faith in Christ's resurrection.

MUSICAL NOTATION

Gregorian Chant may have been the first music to be written down. Its horizontal bars with dots showing the rising and falling notes evolved into the more complex notation system of today.

KEY NOTES

In 1994, recordings of Gregorian Chants from a Spanish monastery rose to No.3 on the U.S. pop album charts and stayed in the top 100 for almost 50 weeks.

JOSEPH HAYDN *1732–1809*

The Creation

THE HEAVENS ARE TELLING THE GLORY OF GOD

This joyous chorus forms the conclusion to the first part of Haydn's great oratorio. Sun, moon and stars, rain, clouds and snow, the continents and the seas, the grass and the trees—all have been included in his musical picture of God's work during the first four days of creation. Then Haydn brings in this glorious chorus, featuring archangels Gabriel, Uriel, and Raphael, characterized by soprano, tenor, and bass. An exuberant orchestra provides a rousing accompaniment to their ecstatic song of praise as they view God's work.

A DEVOUT WORK

The text for Haydn's oratorio, *The Creation*, was written in both English and German. The original was by a forgotten English composer, Thomas Linley, who used the story of Genesis, the first book of the Bible, and John Milton's epic poem, *Paradise Lost*. Haydn, whose English was not fluent, had the text translated into German by his friend, Gottfried van Swieten, an amateur musician and Director of the Court Library in Vienna. Through long hours of

Blind poet John Milton dictates Paradise Lost *to his two daughters.*

dedication and guidance from van Swieten, Haydn prepared more drafts for *The Creation* than any other of his works. He noted: "Never before was I so devout as when I composed *The Creation*. Every day I fell to my knees to pray to God to give me strength."

HAYDN AND NAPOLEON

In 1809, when Napoleon captured Vienna, Haydn was old and ill. The bombardment of the city caused him great suffering. When the house next door was hit by a cannonball, Napoleon—a great admirer of Haydn—placed guards outside the composer's house to protect him. But Haydn still got up every day and played the Austrian national anthem on his piano, as a mark of defiance.

Napoleon (center) defeated the Austrians at the Battle of Marengo in 1800.

KEY NOTES

Eighteen mounted guards and 12 policemen had to protect Haydn from his enthusiastic admirers at the first performance of The Creation *in Vienna, in 1798.*

GREGORIO ALLEGRI *1582–1652*

Miserere

PSALM 51

The *Miserere* is a setting of Psalm 51, "Be merciful to me, O God, because of your constant love." A vaulted nave provides perfect acoustics for such a piece. Allegri wrote it in 1638 for the papal choir of the Sistine Chapel. It is still sung there during Holy Week—the week before Easter Sunday— in a service known as *Tenebrae* (darkness). Evoking the shadow that descended when Jesus died, it is performed in total darkness, with the pope and cardinals kneeling before the altar. Sung by a quartet of soloists and a five-part choir, the contemplative piece is celebrated for the demanding and spine-chilling top Cs sung by the treble. This music was considered so precious that access to the score was restricted and anyone found copying the work could be excommunicated.

SINGER, COMPOSER

Born in 1582, Gregorio Allegri (*left*) was a chorister for nine
years at San Luigi dei Francesi, the French National Church in
Rome, which is famed for its paintings by Caravaggio. In 1600, Allegri
began studying with the famous teacher Giovanni Maria Nanino, before
moving in 1607 to become a chorister and composer at the cathedrals of
Tivoli and then Fermo, on the east coast of Italy. He returned to Rome
to become choirmaster at the hospital church of Santo Spirito. The peak
of his already illustrious career
came when he joined the papal
choir in the Sistine Chapel in
1629, as a singer and composer
under Pope Urban VIII. Allegri died in Rome on
February 7, 1652, at the age of 69.

THE SISTINE CHAPEL

The official private chapel of the pope, the
Sistine Chapel (*right*) takes its name from
Pope Sixtus IV, who had it built in Rome
between 1473 and 1481. Constructed to the dimensions
of the biblical Temple of Solomon (approx. 133 x 44
ft.), its original simple ceiling was transformed in 1508
when Julius II commissioned the great artist
Michelangelo to redecorate it. After painting *The
Creation* and the early history of the world from the
book of Genesis, the artist adorned the huge east wall
of the chapel with his masterpiece, *The Last Judgement*.

PAPAL ROME

In Allegri's day, Rome was the center of a large territory ruled by the pope as an independent state, spreading across central Italy from coast to coast. Its power often led it into conflict, including the terrible Sack of Rome in 1527 by the army of the Holy Roman Emperor, Charles V (*left*), when over 4,000 Roman citizens were slaughtered. The most powerful pope of the time was Urban VIII, who held office from 1623 to 1644. Although more of a warrior prince than a religious leader, he founded several religious orders, the most famous being the Sisters of Mercy.

View from St. Peter's Cathedral in Rome over the famous square, bracketed by Bernini's magnificent colonnades.

THE RISE OF POLYPHONY

The word "polyphony" comes from Greek *polyphonos*, meaning many sounds, and refers to music, such as the *Miserere*, which uses more than one melodic line at the same time. From the 9th century, polyphony grew in complexity. By the Renaissance, composers were writing intricate polyphonic music, weaving many strands of melody. *Spem in Alium* ("Sing and Glorify") by the Englishman Thomas Tallis (1505–1585) is one of the most famous, with 40 such parts, or voices, to it.

A 15th-century polyphonic setting for a mass.

KEY NOTES

For years, Allegri's Miserere was not published, for fear of excommunication. At age 14, Mozart copied it perfectly from memory, earning him much praise, and the ban was lifted.

SERGEI RACHMANINOV *1873–1943*

Vespers

OPUS 37: AVE MARIA

*R*achmaninov wrote his second major choral work, *Vespers*, in 1915. It is acclaimed by many as one of the grandest accomplishments of Russian Orthodox Church music. Vespers are traditionally sung in the Russian Church on the eve of a great feast, an experience much loved by Tchaikovsky, who composed his own version in 17 parts. In Rachmaninov's setting, made up of 15 parts, the mood is contemplative throughout. In part six, the "Ave Maria"—a hymn worshipping the Mother of God—the choir steals in gently and rises to an outburst of praise before falling back, the last peaceful notes slowly dying away.

SACRED TRADITIONS

Russian Orthodox Church music centers on a long tradition of unaccompanied works for choir. The best-known text to be set by both Rachmaninov and Tchaikovsky is the Liturgy of St. John Chrysostom (347–407), Bishop of Constantinople.

KEY NOTES

Rachmaninov once met Charlie Chaplin, an atheist, and asked, "How can you have art without religion?" Chaplin replied, "Art is a feeling more than a belief." The composer retorted, "So is religion!"

GEORGE FRIDERIC HANDEL *1685–1759*

Messiah

I KNOW THAT MY REDEEMER LIVETH

The third part of *Messiah* opens with this famous piece. After exploring Christ's sufferings, Handel concentrates on the Resurrection and the triumph over death. This aria is based on two biblical verses from the Book of Job— the first book in the Bible to contemplate resurrection—and I Corinthians. Written for soprano, this is the soloist's most moving moment in the work and, for many singers, it provides a chance to show skills of ornamentation. One of Handel's best, it is introduced on strings and is a peaceful aria, which hits its peak in its key phrase, "For now is Christ risen."

HANDEL'S UNIVERSAL APPEAL

Handel's *Messiah* has been loved ever since its first performance in 1742. Popular throughout Europe, its fame quickly spread to America, where it was first performed in 1770, and is still sung every Christmas Eve in Boston's Symphony Hall. Despite *Messiah's* far-reaching appeal, the greatest performances of the work have taken place in England. The year 1791 saw 1,068 singers join forces for the oratorio at the Handel Commemoration and, by 1883, numbers at the regular Crystal Palace performance (*right, in 1905*) had swelled to a throng of 4,500 performers, including a 500-piece orchestra. Such spectacular numbers were not achieved again until 1920, when 2,500 singers were brought from the towns of Leeds, Huddersfield and Sheffield to augment the London forces.

A REVERED COMPOSER

In the eyes of some composers, Handel (*left*) was a god. Haydn, driven to tears by the *Hallelujah Chorus*, said, "He is the master of us all," and Mozart re-orchestrated a number of his works, among them *Messiah*. Beethoven, the proud owner of a complete edition of Handel's works, called him "the greatest composer that ever lived." Berlioz, it seems, was alone in his dismissive opinion, calling Handel "a tub of lard and beer."

KEY NOTES

Using one of the names of Jesus as a title for a piece of music was considered blasphemous by some. This may explain why, prior to its London premiere in March 1743, Handel referred to *Messiah* simply as "a new sacred oratorio."

MAURICE DURUFLÉ *1902–1986*

Requiem

OPUS 9: SANCTUS

Traditionally the "Sanctus" offers an opportunity for exciting choral writing. Duruflé, like Fauré before him, makes it a peaceful movement. Around three minutes long, it is the shortest episode in his *Requiem*. Above rippling music played on strings, woodwind and organ, the choir repeats "Sanctus, sanctus, sanctus" ("Holy, holy, holy") three times, becoming gradually more passionate. In the second section, "Hosannah" is repeated until the full choir reaches a short climax on the phrase "in excelsis" ("in the highest"). The music ends in an atmosphere of tranquillity.

OTHER VERSIONS

Duruflé wrote several versions of his *Requiem*: with just organ accompaniment, or with a full or reduced orchestra. The latter consists of organ and strings, and is exactly suited to a solemn, religious occasion.

LIFE OF DURUFLÉ

Maurice Duruflé was born in Louviers, France, in 1902 and, at the age of ten, became a pupil in the choir school in nearby Rouen. In 1919, he left for Paris to study under the organist Charles Tournemire, before entering the Paris Conservatoire the following year. In 1930, after great success in his studies, he was appointed organist at St. Etienne-du-Mont in Paris (*below*), where he stayed until his death in 1986. Professor of Harmony at the Paris Conservatoire from 1943 to 1969, Duruflé wrote one undisputed masterpiece, the *Requiem*. Fiercely self-critical, he rejected much of his own music. He even left the *Requiem* out for the garbage collector, but luckily, it was retrieved.

FRENCH SPECIALITY

The French tradition of building organs and producing music for the instrument dates back to medieval times. The golden age of French organ music was undoubtedly the late 1800s. This was due to the compositions of César Franck and the technical advances made by the famous organ builder Aristide Cavaillé-Coll.

Among the new generation of organists emerging at this exciting time was the partially sighted Louis Vierne (*above*), who became one of Duruflé's most influential teachers.

KEY NOTES

In 1937, Duruflé was at Vierne's side during his last recital at Notre Dame in Paris. The old master was in the middle of a piece when he collapsed and died. Duruflé observed that it was exactly how Vierne wanted his life to end.

WOLFGANG AMADEUS MOZART *1756–1791*

Exsultate, jubilate

K165/158A

This, one of Mozart's most joyful works, is a fine example of the exuberant bravura style so popular in 18th-century Italian church music. The first performance took place at Milan's Theatine Church on January 16, 1773. With the Italian taste for virtuoso solos in mind, the 16-year-old Mozart incorporated every opportunity for soloists to show off their skills in this motet. From the rousing introduction to the final triumphant "Allelujah," the work is a display of sparkling brilliance. Even during the slower central section, the music never flags. The piece ends with a jubilant flourish, in as lively a manner as it began.

IMPERIAL DELAY

In 1772, Mozart and his father, Leopold, visited Milan—where *Exsultate, jubilate* was written—to attend the premiere of his latest opera *Lucio Silla*, based on events in ancient Rome. Commissioned for performance at the 1772 Milanese Carnival season, the opera was composed to a text by Giovanni de Gamerra, the music-loving Governor General of Lombardy. The greatest opera singers of the day were procured for the production of the opera, but the premiere—which was due to take place before the Emperor of Austria—was delayed for three hours until his arrival and did not end until 2 a.m. Twenty-six more performances were given during Mozart's stay in Milan, but the opera was not seen again until 1929, when it was staged in Prague.

Milan Cathedral, center of a strong tradition of religious music dating back to the 4th century.

SCOURGE OF MUNICH

Mozart wrote both the solo in *Exsultate, jubilate* and Cecelio's solo in *Lucio Silla* for the castrato Venanzio Rauzzini (1746–1810). Despite his physical deficiencies, Rauzzini (*right*) once had to flee Munich for seducing the wives of several noblemen! In 1774, he moved to England, becoming famous as a singer in London, before moving to Bath, where he lived in an Italian-styled cottage and received musical guests such as Joseph Haydn.

KEY NOTES

When he couldn't decide which musical phrase to use in a composition, Mozart sometimes threw dice to choose between the alternatives.

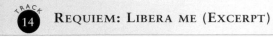
GIUSEPPE VERDI *1813–1901*

Requiem

LIBERA ME (EXCERPT)

This is the final part of Verdi's dramatic *Requiem* for four solo voices, choir and full orchestra. This section opens with a soprano soaring on the word "requiem" in a high, pure tone over a quiet, yet ominous choral accompaniment. Announced by warning phrases on strings, she moves into a passionate plea for deliverance from eternal death, *"libera me"* ("deliver me"), made all the more striking by thunderous echoes on drums and brass. Here the *Requiem* shows its operatic qualities, almost like one of Verdi's dramatic death scenes. Finally, the soprano calmly repeats her plea on a single note to bring the passage to its end.

VERDI'S HERO

When Gioachino Rossini died in 1868, Verdi proposed that leading Italian composers collaborate on a requiem in his memory. Each composer was to write a different movement, Verdi's task being to compose the "Libera me." Sadly, plans for a performance in San Pietrino, Bologna, failed when the opera house refused to lend singers or orchestra without payment. But Verdi eventually found a use for the music. He was moved by the death of the great Italian poet, Alessandro Manzoni (*left*), and vowed to honor his hero. The Mayor of Milan accepted Verdi's offer of a requiem mass. In the final work—first performed in San Marco, Milan, on May 22, 1874—the composer included his earlier "Libera me."

THE UNIFICATION OF ITALY

In the 19th century, the desire for Italian unity reached its peak. For centuries, Italy had been made up of numerous states, centered around powerful cities such as Venice, Rome, and Turin. The kings of Piedmont in northern Italy led the drive for unity, forcing the Austrians out of Lombardy in 1859. The following year, the famous patriot Garibaldi captured Sicily and Naples. In 1861, the Italian Kingdom was proclaimed and Victor Emmanuel II of Piedmont (*above, right, meeting Garibaldi*) was crowned king. Florence was the capital until Rome was captured in 1870, when the unification was complete.

KEY NOTES

British soprano Lynne Dawson sang part of the "Libera me" at Princess Diana's funeral at Westminster Abbey in 1997.

Credits &
Acknowledgments

PICTURE CREDITS

Cover /Title and Contents Pages/ IBC: Images Colour Library; Bridgeman Art Library, London/British Library, London 2, 16, Private Collection (George Fennel Robson: Loch Katrine) 3(l), The De Morgan Foundation (Evelyn de Morgan: Visitation, Virgin Mary & Elizabeth) 3(r), Giraudon/Koninklijk Museum voor Schone Kunste, Antwerp (Rogier van der Weyden: The Seven Sacraments Altarpiece) 4, Heimatmuseum, Kothen 9(tr), Palazzo Medici-Ricciardi, Florence (Benozzo Gozzoli; Angels in a Heavenly Landscape) 10, Giraudon/National Museum of Ancient Art, Lisbon (Taborda Vlame Carlos: Four Angels Playing Instruments) 12, Giraudon/Chateau de Versailles (Louis Lejeune: The Battle of Marengo (detail) 13(r), Cider House Galleries, Bletchingley (Leon Bortarel: Milton Composing Poetry) 13(l), Vatican Museums & Galleries, Rome 15(r), Fitzwilliam Museum, University of Cambridge (Master of the Magdalen Legend: Charles V) 16(tl), Kremlin Museums, Moscow 17, Museo di San Marco dell'Angelico, Florence (Fra Angelico: The Resurrection) 18, Giraudon/Musée d'Orsay (Claude Monet: Rouen Cathedral in Full Sunlight) 20, Giraudon 21(l), Galleria dell'Accademia, Florence (Luigi Mussini: Sacred Music) 22, Phillips, the International Fine Art Auctioneers (William Wyld: Milan Cathedral) 23(l); E.T. Archive: 5(b), 9(bl), 25(b); Mary Evans Picture Library: 9(br), 25(t); Fine Art Photographic Library/Private Collection (Léon l'Hermite: Good Friday) 6, (Franz Richard Unterberger: In a Monastery Garden) 11; Images Colour Library: 8, 16(bl), 24; Lebrecht Collection: 5(t), 15(l), 19(l & r) 21(r), 23(r); The Stock Market: 14.

All illustrations and symbols: John See